BORN ON A BED OF GRACE

Published by Spines
ISBN: 979-8-89383-186-3

BORN ON A BED OF GRACE

ANNIE P. RIVERS

DEDICATION

This book is dedicated to Almighty God Jehovah through Christ Jesus with the help of the Holy Spirit!!!

To my children: Aisha, Seanardo, and Shimere; my grandchildren; great-grandchildren; and my siblings: Gloria, Sandra, Richard, Darryel, Donald, and David (Terrell).

CONTENTS

ACKNOWLEDGMENTS

I would like to thank Larry D. Thomas for his words of encouragement, "Write it, I'll read it." Thanks to Robin Chappell-Thompson for reigniting my love for writing during her "30-Day Writing Challenge." Lastly, to Spines for making my dreams a reality.

EARLY YEARS

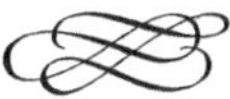

Well, after all the procrastination, excuses, and plain disobedience; I have finally sat down to write this book as Almighty God has commanded me. I cannot say that I know exactly where I am headed with my thoughts as God would have them, but I trust the Holy spirit to guide me. One place I think I will begin is with my childhood and how I viewed my world early on in life. To start, my mom and dad were separated as early as I can remember from age 3 or earlier. I am the oldest of four during the earlier years of my mother's separation from my father, that is, three daughters were born out of their union and later my mother gave birth to my brother. You see, in those days it was not unusual for a separated or divorced woman to live with her parents, her children, and her only sister. There were some struggles from time to time because my grandfather was a weekend drinker and gambler and all that accompanied that lifestyle, while the rest of the family was living as Jehovah's Witnesses (JW). Looking back over my life, poverty is very real, that is, lacking food, utilities shut off, poor housing conditions, and roller coaster finances. I must say it is very hard on a child, mainly, because the child doesn't understand the costs of living and why they must go lacking in anything. This is especially true when adults leave the house every day to go to work. In my case, I saw my grandfather, grandmother, and mother leave for work. My grandfather worked for a memorial company, pouring cement for headstones, burial slabs, and monuments. Of course, on days that it rained; he was unable to work. However, my grandmother and mother worked a few days out of the week as housemaids. Therefore, whatever dollars they were able to make, left no room for my grandfather's weekend drinking and gambling... he was paid on Fridays unless it was a holiday or something. I do not know if my grandmother or mother was paid by more than one homeowner or not doing the week. Either way, I am sure granddaddy made most of the money. Likewise, the family was depending on my grandfather's wages the most. It would be heartbreaking to look forward to a planned shopping day for food and/or clothing and that's the time granddaddy squandered the money. Now, my grandmother, mother, and aunt (who received money weekly for washing and ironing granddaddy's clothes and money from my mother for babysitting my siblings and me) had to scrape up money between them to buy food, shoes, or whatever.

Granddaddy Squandered The Money

Ironically, it took years for me to figure out why we never seemed to have enough money, yet the adults were getting paid. Honestly, the grown-ups never discussed bills in front of the children, therefore, I never had a clue how much the rent or utilities were until my grandfather passed in January 2000. Granddaddy's drinking and gambling were at their worst during my pre-school year to first grade (1960-1961). I remember when I was 6 years old, one Saturday afternoon, grandaddy came home after staying out all night. I was happy to see him drive up, as I announced, "Granddaddy's here!" No one seemed to care, especially the adults. I greeted him and welcomed him into the house. He didn't receive attention from my grandmother nor did my aunt acknowledge his presence. There had to be something wrong because my grandmother did not get up to fix him a plate nor did my aunt offer to do so. Surely, being the helpful little girl I was, I asked him if he was hungry, and I offered to fry him an egg. He ate it with left over grits w/hot sauce and bread, along with syrup as I recalled. Interestingly, as he ate, he began to say how everyone was mad at him and did not love him anymore. That's when I reassured him, that I loved him. He soon went to bed after that. I remember asking, "Why did nobody fix Granddaddy something to eat?"

My grandmother replied, saying something to this effect, "If it had been left up to him, it wouldn't have been anything to eat."

And that is when I learned my granddaddy had been the culprit all along. That was quite an eye-opener, he received no more pep talks from me. He was forced to look at himself. The gambling eventually came to a halt, while his weekend drinking continued.

What's Biting My Foot?

The more I think about it, having the utilities shut off ranks number 2 in comparison to being hungry. I felt very uneasy whenever the power was shut off because of nonpayment; however, knowing the power could be restored along with the neighbors was a greater consolation, even though I disliked having anything shut off in our home. I remember times when the gas was off, and we had to cook and warm up water on a "hot plate" to bathe. I recall an incident when our gas was shut off. We had eaten, watched TV, and were getting ready to go to bed. Every night we kneeled on the side of the bed (my mother, 2 younger sisters, baby brother, and me) and repeated the Lord's Prayer before climbing into bed with my mother. Of course, as the oldest, our ages ranged from 7, 6.5, and 5, to youngest at 4.5 years old. This particular night we got into our usual sleeping order, that is, my mother on one side of the bed and I on the other side with my siblings in between. I felt something tugging at my foot from underneath the covers. Every time I pulled my foot back into bed underneath the covers, this thing would pull my foot out again while nibbling on my big toe. I called out to my mother saying, "something is biting my foot." Like anything else, she thinking I'm being dramatic about something biting my foot, tells me, "There is nothing biting your foot, now go to sleep."

So, I see it's going to take some acting skills to get her attention. I say, in my urgent whining voice, "Something is biting my foot."

My mother gets up and turns on the light, naturally, it runs away.

I try and explain what foot is being attacked and how this thing is biting me and pulling my foot out of bed. I suggested keeping the lights on. That did not go over well, and the lights were turned off. Two minutes later, I am really stirred up because shaking and kicking my foot isn't helping at all. So, this time I want my mother to turn on the light so I can check my foot. She turns them on and I exam my foot, I shout, "it's bleeding, my toe is bleeding." My mother then rushed over to look. When she was done with my foot, I realized it wasn't my blood. According to my mother's conclusion, it was candy/something sweet on my foot that had been sniffed and nibbled on by a rat. Geesh! My, My, My! I can remember so many stories while we lived in that house, on that street, in that impoverished neighborhood in the 1960s. I would like to title this next story…

When Was The Last Time You Seen Your Daddy?

OMG, when I tell you my sisters and I have heard this statement over a million times, just believe it anyway, because it certainly feels like it while growing up and well into our adulthood. It really did not matter where we saw them or who they were, if they knew my father, their very next question after affirming our names and ages was, "when was the last time you saw your daddy?" Why were they asking little kids this question? Surely, you know the answer to that question better than us.

Perhaps we should be asking you that question. Could it be you saw him last, and he told you when he last saw us? Believe it or not, I felt like some of these people were being insensitive to inquire. Many times, we didn't answer like his three girls, we allowed my mother to answer. Only a sensitive person would have known that question made us sad inside and it felt like we were being made fun of or the butt of somebody's joke or gossip. In other words, were your intentions to see us or to add salt to our unhealed wounds? As time went on, we noticed as adults with our own families, people continued to ask that same question. This was a question embedded in our thoughts, therefore, we decided to have some fun with it. We would randomly ask each other, "when was the last time you saw your daddy?" As if we really cared and laughing... that laughing was so therapeutic for our soul. We later used it as a running joke, briefly, for our amusement and to see the reaction of our children. Thanking God, we took the sting, hurt, embarrassment, and confusion out of the question.

A Wooden House Dust And Asthma

Living in that old wooden grey shotgun house was never a dull moment. My folk noticed whenever the weather changed suddenly or dust, allergens, and pollen filled the air, my baby brother would start wheezing. Most of the time my mother was able to head off an attack of asthma bronchitis, a condition in which it is difficult to breathe because of inflamed air passages. During that time my mother was told it was a great chance that he would grow out of the condition. There were random nights when my mother sat up with my little brother rocking him applying vapor rub to his chest and pinning a cloth to his under shirt to keep the ointment close and effectively using his body heat. During days or nights of wheezing, it could get scary watching my baby brother struggle to breathe with his eyes looking stretched and glossy with fear and anxiety. The nights were the hardest, I would be so sleepy but afraid to go to sleep without him showing signs of getting better. Oh, my! I will never forget a night my brother was wheezing so bad and looking so uncomfortable, I had not experienced seeing him look so helpless before. I kept praying that he would feel relief and couldn't see enough improvement to be satisfied that he was getting better. Likewise, as I watched him struggle, I became sad and afraid for him. I asked my mother if my brother was going to die. She nervously shouted out, "No, he's not going to die!" I cannot tell you how those words reassured me. Perhaps, those words eased him too. Not long afterward, say about an hour, my brother's breathing was improving. The next morning, my mother informed me that she would be going to work shortly; however, I would be going with my little brother to the doctor's office (located in one of the local hospitals where his dad worked as a cook). In addition, his father would be picking us up in a cab, so make sure we were dressed and ready to go when he arrived. Although my brother knew his father, he stayed close to me. He was about 4 and I was 8 years old. I told him we were going to the doctor, so he could feel better. He replied, "Okay."

Once we got to the doctor's office, my brother's dad introduced us. I made certain I answered the health professionals' questions and described the asthma attacks as they occurred. During a particular procedure (breathing treatment) I assisted my brother. Unfamiliar with that technique, he leaned over and asked me, "Am I going to die?"

Remembering that stern answer I got from my mother, I said, "No, you are NOT going to die. That's just some medicine to help you breathe better, Okay!?"

He replied, "Okay." Looking at me with pure confidence in his eyes, as I smiled and held his hand. At that moment, I did not notice my brother and I were being observed. However, a nurse, the doctor, and my brother's dad were present. The nurse asked, "What did he ask you?" I replied, "He asked me if he was going to die." That's when I gave her and those nearby my reassuring response. I believe all eyes got watery after that reply. I was told by the nurse, "You're a good big sister!" To which, I replied, "Thank you!" Looking lovingly and proudly at my brother. I was given instructions by the health professionals to tell and give my mother (my brother's dad assured the professionals I could follow their instructions, as they agreed). My brother and I returned home with him at peace because he had been seen by the professionals. And as for me, I had another opportunity to be proud of myself and gain more status from my mom.

I Did Not Know My Father When I Saw Him Again

I have found it to be very interesting that the absent parent is usually looked upon by a child or children as a faultless parent. That is, for whatever reason they are not presence, it's okay. In contrast, the present parent is controlling, has no fun, doesn't understand, and needs to loosen up a little. Somehow, I only thought of positive things for my father. Reality would soon visit my little world of denial. Still quite young, my mother, grandmother, siblings, and I were taking a nice summer evening drive, when we came across this community that my family once lived in and attended school, church, and gatherings prior to my birth. There was a store that had been there many years prior and was known as a community hangout. My mother drives up and parks. Now, my sisters, brother, and I are getting excited about the store. Unexpectedly, my mother says, "There's y'all, Daddy."

I said, "Where? I don't see him." My mother makes mention of the direction in which he is standing and says he went inside the store. Now, she tells my sisters and me to go into the store together and say hello. We went inside, I started looking around this large store and got separated from my sisters. I called out their names, and I went from aisle to aisle looking. I'm sure I was probably noticed on the circular security mirror. The store was quiet, so I decided to exit. On my way out, a strange-looking man stood at the opposite end of the aisle. He looked nothing like the pictures I've seen. That is when I decided it was time to leave; however, on my way out I heard a man say, "Hey!" I ran back to the car, telling my mother, "I didn't see him." Sadly, my mother refused to go with me and did not allow one of my sisters to go with me. Therefore, I went back into the store. This time I was met at the door and asked, what do I want? In my mind, I want every toy I could ever dream of having. So much was before me on the walls, what looked like colorful toys were not... something practical to use to complete tasks. I asked the store cashier if they had a rack rack paddle. She replied, "No." I was asked if I wanted chips or candy. I wanted a toy; I couldn't remember receiving anything from my father… I needed a monumental gift. I finally got tired of looking and asked the cashier for some large balloons for a party. Perhaps, I thought I could make up for lost time in 20 awkward, unattached minutes. I don't know what was most disappointing, not getting a meaningful toy or receiving a single red balloon and not a pack of balloons.

As I walked back to the car, I felt down, somehow disappointed. Why didn't my father help me pick out a toy??? Oh, but it gets worse. My mother asked, "What did you get, Pearl?"

I, boldly, answered, "I got a balloon."

My mother said, "A balloon. You should have asked for something to eat."

I strongly replied, "I didn't want anything to eat, I wanted a toy." I don't know if that ever made sense to Mother, Daddy, or the cashier; but one thing I do know in my hearts of hearts. I knew my grandmother understood, for me, that was all that mattered. Reflecting, as a child I could say my father bought me a red balloon. This story was so sad on many levels: I did not know my father or how he looked, and he did not know me, especially, my heart and thoughts of him as the absent parent. I must say, reality soon kicked in afterward, I learned quickly that my absent parent was not the ideal parent and needed to appreciate my mother more.

When We Moved To The Projects, It Was Like Heaven Sent

I don't know how many people would admit this, but in the 1960s it was a blessing to get an apartment in the projects. My family and I considered it heaven sent, because the old wooden houses were very cold in the winter, in fact, one little space heater usually occupied a room. There would be times we had to close off the hallway to keep a room warm. Putting on extra clothes to stay warm. The idea of someone having to go out of the room to the kitchen, bathroom, or outside was torture, mainly, because the cold air would sail into the room removing all hope of future warmth. Another blessed reason, my family qualified for government programs, such as reduced rent, school lunches, and food stamps that required we pay a cash fee first, to receive them. The apartment was so nice and crispy warm, one large heater in the living room heated the entire 2 story apartment. We received a 3-bedroom apartment with a washer outlet and a large food pantry. The gas, water/garbage were included in the rent, meaning, soothing hot baths any time of day or night. No more warming water or gas shut-offs. My, that alone, kept me in a place of gratitude because our rent was being paid on time. Granddaddy continued to drink on weekends, if working, he drank when he got off. I believe gambling was not heavy in his life anymore, he brought home the money every week and helped with all of the house expenses. And to top my gratitude list off even more, there were no rodents coming inside our home. Management routinely scheduled pest control in and outside the apartment. What may not have meant much to anyone else at that time in the '60s, I saw our move to the housing project as heaven-sent, and guess what? I treated it that way until it wasn't heaven anymore.

Trouble Came Against What Heaven Sent

You may be asking yourself, what could have possibly come against their heaven-sent blessing. Well, as I look back on it, the opposition did not happen all at once. Follow me, as I fill you in on the details. My granddaddy owned a car, and it was ok, but sometimes we wanted to go places and grandaddy wasn't around. So, my mother and grandmother decided to get a car for my mother to drive. We got the car, we were able to visit, go for drives, go out of town, shop, etc. However, while we were praising Jehovah for another awesome blessing, jealousy was brewing in the neighborhood. It was a car, many neighbors had them that could drive. This particular evening, when we arrived home after being gone most of the day, we could hear someone sarcastically say, "They think they are rich," among the many sitting on their porches watching us arrive home. Of course, if they thought they could intimidate us, they learned early they were wrong. My mother and grandmother walked with their heads up, whether they had a dollar or not, and always a smile on their faces. They taught my siblings and me the same. I don't have to tell anyone, just know, that I was a force to be reckoned with all by myself, LOL Interestingly, time went on, and my grandmother was asked to go to the manager's office. The management said someone told them we had a new car, and they wanted to know whose car it was and how much it cost. Next, management started going up on the rent frequently without notice. While telling my grandmother, that our neighbors said we didn't need housing authority because we were rich, and we were always buying something new for the apartment. My folks agreed that if they could pay such an outrageous amount for rent, then why not pay that amount in a mortgage for a house? Our jealous neighbors were only preparing us for greater because every time they raised the rent,

Jehovah met my family's needs, no matter what it was. As a matter of fact, my mother was dating an Elder from the Kingdom Hall of Jehovah's Witnesses at the time. I don't know, but perhaps, the thought of my mother marrying an eligible man is what sent our neighbors into an uncontrollable envy and bitterness.

Likewise, my gratitude grew, and I was so grateful that my mother and grandmother were serious about loving God. As long as I can remember, my family were Jehovah's Witnesses. Therefore, that was the only religion I ever knew from preschool to 12th grade. We were taught to study our Bibles, engage in family, and group bible studies, and participate in the Theocratic Ministry School where I was taught by my mother to write and execute a sermon in skits-like presentations from the age of 8 and thus prepare sermons on my own at 10. We went from house to house, known as field service, engaging in short discussions taught during our weekly theocratic ministry school. I was 5 years old when I learned to go from house to house presenting the Watchtower and Awake magazines with my mom for a small contribution of 10 cents for both magazines. I watched as my mother, grandmother, and aunt fell deeply in love with Jehovah in the good, bad, and difficult times… not wavering at all. This love for God sparked something deep inside of me. So, I thirsted and hungered after him with everything inside me because I knew he loved me without a doubt. On this incredible walk with him, I learned to pray out of my many examples. It was then I learned God answered prayers from getting A's on a test to landing great summer jobs each year. When I reached junior high, my mom got engaged to marry one of the ministers, he was divorced without children and found my mom to be the woman for him. His intention was to make a family with her and her four children. When I look back, we were fond of him when they were courting, up until he popped the question. I felt he would be taking our absent father's place in our lives, like really!? I remember my sisters and I washing our school sweaters in the bathtub for the week, amid all of the splashing, I heard my mom tell my grandmother and aunt that her suitor just might be popping the question soon. That is when I initiated the protest for my siblings and me, unfortunately, at the time they couldn't care less. So, I stepped up to voice my objection to my mother, "He's not going to be my daddy."

She came back firmly saying, "He's not going to be your daddy, he's going to be my husband!"

That is when I threw my heavy wet sweater back into the water with great force and anger, only to have her come to the bathroom door to check if there was a problem. I must say, sure enough, he proposed that evening and she said, "Yes." I got over it as I watched her get married at my junior high school community center… she was so beautiful, and I could honestly see they were in love. Turned out, he was the best dad ever… three amazing brothers were born out of that union. Some years later, "Daddy Jack," as we affectionally called him passed, and my siblings (the first group of us) were extremely saddened by his death. He provided well for my mother and brothers, just as he promised he would do. They were happy serving God and doing life together.

NEWFOUND FREEDOM AND HOW DISOBEDIENCE ALMOST TOOK ME OUT

What a joy it was to become a teenager in high school and not have to be treated like a child by my mother. That was the moment of appreciation for my newfound freedom. I felt like I knew what it was to be responsible, and I was going to prove to my family that I was right on track. Wow, we held a small group of Tuesday night bible studies in our home for many years, therefore, our moving did not change our schedule. My parents (mother and new father) picked us up every Thursday night for the Kingdom Hall (church) and on Sundays. Everything was going well for my siblings and me as we enjoyed living with my grandparents without all the strictness of my mother. However, I can assure you my mother still reigned as queen in our discipline from her household. Amazing enough, the house rules had no bearing on our living arrangement, they were written in stone. For instance, we could only attend family and members functions (baby showers, weddings, conventions, special services, get-togethers, etc.); no sleepovers; could not participate in school sports; no dating; did not celebrate birthdays or holidays; and could not attend the school's proms. Honestly, the first two years (9/1970-5/1972) were no real problems for me to obey, because my mother was still near to reinforce her disciplinary skills and position. I maintained good grades, especially in health occupations and physical education... those classes piqued my interest a great deal. I loved the medical field and its scientific expressions concerning the body and its functions. The same was true for sports i.e. basketball, flag football, softball; field & track; stunts & tumbles on the trampoline; and volleyball. I asked my mother for permission to join the school's basketball team, I was told "no" each year. I felt deprived of the opportunities to enjoy my life as a teenager, and I wanted more. That's when my siblings (the girls) and I decided we would do as much as possible to enjoy our friends in the neighborhood without going overboard. We started by asking our friends to ask my grandmother if we could have a short visit with them at our house and later at their homes. In the beginning, my grandmother was hesitant about us going to others' homes without contacting my mother; however, my mother did not have a phone at the time. Of course, as time continued to pass, we were able to visit until the streetlights came on. Later, we started getting invited to parties held at night. Just know, this was on another level and the permission to attend a night neighborhood party was going to be very unlikely to definitely not. Therefore, in order to combat that decision of being told "no" my youngest sister broke ground by leaving out of the bedroom window when no one was watching and returning to a locked window, compliments of myself. It was after my middle sister and I heard the details of her experience, that we considered the risks. However, it wasn't long afterward, that my grandmother discovered my youngest sister was not in the house, that's when my sister and I were given the assignment to escort her back home. Now, this is when we discovered the "fun" of a neighborhood party. I was able to get a dance in at two not one party. My sister and I took so long to get back home until my grandmother stood and noted me being cheered on while dancing... I had gotten a dose of that party fever and it was on for me. I remember, my sisters and I planned our own party version in our back yard, that is, we got together with friends for refreshments (chips, hot dogs, sodas, dip, etc.); we had my brother's music box; to our surprise, and quite a few people attended. It was fun and we were surprised at the crowd we had gathered. On another note, perhaps, the party was too loud for my grandmother's comfort, because after that night she did not mind the party being held elsewhere, lol.

Interestingly enough, dating was the next rule of the house that needed to be addressed. I remained a virgin in my sophomore and junior years of high school; however, I had plenty of male friends that I enjoyed interacting with in school and during school activities i.e. pep rallies, football games, field trips, etc., as well. There were times when I would allow a guy to have my number after watching and getting to know him better. I was introduced to a guy who was a year ahead of me. He asked if he could come over to my house, by now, I am a junior in high school. I mentioned to my grandmother that I had invited this friend of mine to our house for a couple of hours. Interesting to note, back in the day (70's) it was not unusual for a guy to come over on a Wednesday night for a couple of hours (school night). Nor was it unusual for those without dates to walk the neighborhood looking to see whose car was in whose driveway, if someone's boyfriend was at someone's else house, and vice versa… just so they, could torment the person on the school bus the next day and call the person a liar for claiming that person. At any rate, I was able to start dating, that is, going to the movies and double dating from time to time. It looked as though my life was reflecting a regular teenager on one hand, and on the other, it reflected a life of religious outdated traditions.

Disobedience Introduced Itself As Fun In My Senior Year Of High School

Living in disobedience became that secret life that took me further than I was prepared to go. I always felt it was my mother's strictness that choked me, but I was wrong, because as long as my siblings and I were covered by her, we were protected. Trying to exhaust my grandmother's authority was working against the foundation of my existence. Meaning, that I knew the life I lived under the protection of my mother was the safest; however, the life I desired, I was unfamiliar, and I lacked knowledge of the true pitfalls that exist behind the scenes.

It is important to note, that it was in my senior year of high school that I began to smoke weed, frequent a particular nightclub on the weekend, and miss school each Monday. It took my Economics/Government class instructor to bring to my attention the obvious pattern I had developed. In fact, she stated it before my classmates, "Rivers, I will see you on Tuesday, because you'll be out on Monday." I do not have to tell you she got my attention quickly. Amazing, just that attention alone from her gave me the authoritative voice I missed and possibly, had been longing for all alone.

Understandably, I was hearing my mother's voice less and I was attempting to drown out my grandmother's voice, as well.

It was then that I decided to get myself together and buckle down in my studies for graduation. I was forced to look at my grades, behaviors, and friends. My choice of friends had gone extremely out of the range of knowledge I was familiar with and the empowerment I needed to dominate life on my own. I was in vast waters without a life jacket how I should stay afloat? Honestly, my right hand did not have a clue of what my left hand was doing in those streets. It was by the grace of God that I graduated on schedule because a "B+" or above was needed on the finals for two of my core classes.

Likewise, I was preparing to go into nursing school in the fall. It was during mid-summer that I discovered I was pregnant after having been on birth control pills for a couple of months. My whole world as I knew it was crashing down, what was I going to do? I remember thinking I have let my entire family down, what are they going to think of me? Likewise, I remember not feeling my best and urinating a lot. I could not stand to smell or taste the grease in burgers, fries, or onions on my food. In fact, the very first time I felt nauseated, my family and I were in Atlanta for a convention. I felt so miserable during our stay in the hotel room, that I shared with my sister after trying to eat my favorite special-ordered hamburger. It never dawned on me I could have been pregnant at that time. I decided I would make an appointment to see a doctor when we returned home.

My Reaction To The Doctor's Diagnosis

I made the appointment to see our primary doctor. He was an older gentleman who talked loudly and could be heard throughout the doctor's office. He was a very good doctor with an affordable fee of $7.00 per visit. When my turn to be examined came, I felt like holding my breath, because everyone would be able to hear my diagnosis, just as I heard others before me. The doctor looked at me and in his "as a matter of fact" the voice said, "You're pregnant."

I replied, "No, I'm not!"

And to that, the doctor says, "Well, I guess you know." That was the end of our conversation. He told the nurse about my unbelief of pregnancy. I'm sure she and the entire office heard everything by the looks on their faces. However, I did not make a follow-up appointment, this was a very big mistake. Fear paralyzed me into believing the circumstances of disobedience could be hoped or wished away, in other words, I have done wrong before and Jehovah covered me. Surely, my God will make everything okay again. Oh my, that did not happen. The pregnancy was on my mind all my waking hours, I could not focus on anything else. My secret consumed me of enjoying life and the future. All I had to look forward to was shame, and unforgiveness from God, family, church folks, and self. Even the embarrassment of having my name read out loud before the congregation that I was disfellowshipped and telling the congregation to treat me as if I did not exist anymore was painful. Meaning, not calling my name or speaking to me ever again, unless I went through the process of a reinstatement. Mercy, who knew what that looked like; especially, when you are told Jehovah God doesn't love you anymore and you have no one to love you, including your family. My family never stopped talking to me and they never stopped loving me. Although, in the past, I saw many family members cut their children, sisters, brothers, and other relatives completely off. Husbands and wives continued their communication with a large hole between them, as their marriages suffered.

The question became, where is God? Does He hate me? Will He still listen to me? Will God ever forgive me once the baby is born? I cried myself to sleep many days and nights. I knew in my heart, there was no way I could live in this world without God's love and protection. I loved God, I needed him, I depended on Him, and He was all I ever had and knew since I was 4 years old or younger. What was I going to do without his help in a time of desperation and trouble? Perhaps, I could have made it without the forgiveness of others for my "wrongs," according to JWs; yet, I could not see myself living on earth a single day, without Jehovah's love and protection. For that reason, I started to believe dying would be the answer to all my problems, besides, I felt God had no use for me on the earth anymore because I disappointed Him… I let God down. In other words, if God could throw you away, according to religion, what is one left to do?

What About The Baby's Father?

Well into my pregnancy, I learned that the young man I lost my virginity to (we always used protection) and was seeing randomly, had several children of his own and even had surgery to prevent having any future children. I never knew about his ongoing relationship until I learned of my pregnancy. However, there was another young man I was sleeping with from time to time that I genuinely loved and loved me. He was in our local college, loved God, and had a promising future in front of him. I decided not to make it known to him that I was pregnant, although we made a point of using protection, my reasoning was I did not want to destroy his future alongside my own. It was years later that I told him of my hidden pregnancy and life-threatening delivery. Needless to say, I had no right to keep the birth of his daughter a secret nor the complications that ensued. In the darkest, most painful, scariest, and loneliest time of my life; I did not know God had a plan to pull me through my chaos and the choices I made for the baby and my life. Today, I understand that my circumstances did not catch God off guard nor were my challenges too perplexed for God's intervention.

What About Nursing School?

I cannot tell you how I was grasping for straws, trying to make my life make sense. That is, trying to bring order to the chaos was fruitless. I applied for nursing school soon after graduation around August of 1973 for Fall 1973 believing I was on my way to a successful, productive life. Yet, in my current condition, I knew I was with a child. Nevertheless, I attended orientation to start school. During my interview, I was asked if there was anything that might limit or restrict my school participation. I replied, "No, I don't think so, I am pregnant though." To my surprise, I wondered why

I was confessing a guarded secret to the instructor anyway.

The nursing instructor's response was, "How far along are you?"

I gave her what I thought was the correct answer, "I'm 3 months."

The instructor replied, "I would suggest you come back after the baby is born. There would be less strain on your body if you wait."

Of course, not going into a debate, I simply agreed to reapply after the baby was born. Likewise, I was extremely disappointed because I did not have anything to aspire to or to normalize my life and add worth. It was in that mind frame I fell into a deep depression. No smiling, no laughter, and no sense of well-being. What about God? I let Him down the most, He was my friend, and based on my religion, God was a punishing God... I felt totally doomed for life and I wanted to die. So, in my desperation I tried taking a bottle of pain relievers to kill myself; instead, I woke up wondering why was I still alive. I knew I would, eventually, go before the elders of the congregation. Noting, my stepfather was an elder too, and I would be declared disfellowshipped in front of him too. Again, that's the procedure of reading a statement before the congregation severing all ties to an individual. Even if you should decide to be reinstated, they are not to talk to you or acknowledge your presence in any way for a set amount of time, i.e... months or years. This being the only religion I had ever known and listening to them say repeatedly this is the only true religion in the world... I was devastated. Not only was I an outsider, but I had also embarrassed my loved ones, God, and self. There was no place for me to turn and no one to come to my aid because I had betrayed my God, according to religion.

Let it be noted, that I agonized over my pregnancy for at least five months before telling anyone. I suffered in silence, hoping the baby would go away. Falling deeper into a dark hole of reoccurring mental and emotional despair. Placing an uncalled judgment over my life that God did not request or ask me to make. Dying on the inside because of what folks may or may not think of me. When reality they wanted to take the place of God without God's permission and His loving kind characteristics. I have learned over the years that Jehovah will always give you a way out. For example, out of the blue, my birth father writes me a letter from prison saying, "Congratulations on your pregnancy, it's a girl." When I got to this part of the letter I said, "How does he know?" Looking franticly over my shoulders, I quickly folded the letter and placed it back in the envelope. My father's gifts from God were dreams and visions. I later found out my mom was afraid of these gifts of "knowing" that my dad carried. Turned out, he would tell her of his dreams over the years, when their path would cross, only for her to say she did not want to hear of his encounters. Today, I believe that incident was meant to ease and relax my mind of my "secret." Just having another significant person in my life to know of my pregnancy, helped me with the overbearing weight that I carried. No matter how shocking and supernaturally the experience presented itself, I was relieved.

I Tried Signing Up For An Unwed Mothers' Home

Of course, not long after my father contacted me, I contacted a lady who worked with unwed pregnant girls. I made an appointment for a representative of the program to come to my home so that I might get a better understanding and be evaluated for placement. I told her of my dilemma with the church folk (Jehovah's Witnesses) and how I was an embarrassment to my family and all that they taught me to be. The time came when I felt the baby move, therefore, denying I was pregnant and needing to be further confirmed by a doctor was no longer an escape route for me. Therefore, I needed a solution, and signing myself over to a home for unwed mothers was a reasonable solution to my problem. Amazingly, at the end of our conversation, the counselor suggested I sit down and tell my folks about my pregnancy. She felt they would understand, as she showed me great compassion and understanding. Cleverly enough, this lady said, that if I talked to my folks about my pregnancy and they wanted me out of the home, give her a callback. Honestly, that was a very clever suggestion, because in my mind I had a place to go and would be calling her back soon. Likewise, because I was 17 at the time, I needed a parent or guardian's signature to be admitted into the home. So, as soon as I entered the house, I asked my grandmother to sign me over to this home for girls she refused. She said, "I ain't signing no papers for you to go nowhere." Somehow, I grew comfort from that because she was not sending me away and she now knew the secret I had been carrying for months. Oh, my what a relief that was, hallelujah!! Okay, walls were being knocked down one by one. However, there was one more hurdle I needed to clear, it was going before the Elders of the congregation (SN: Jehovah's Witnesses hate it when you call their meeting place a "church," they prefer it to be called a Kingdom Hall, congregation, or organization). Nevertheless, the day came when my parents informed the Elders, that I was with a child.

I Went Before The Elders

Honestly, I knew going before the elders would present some form of embarrassment because my stepfather, the man I called daddy for years, would be present as an elder, as well. So, I made it up in my mind, certain questions were not going to be answered. Considering the fact, that I had a best friend who was pregnant, as well, who went before the elders long before me. I asked her what some of the questions were that they asked her, I could not believe how personal they were; yet she answered all of them. Okay, here goes: It was about 7:00 pm on a weeknight, and I arrived at the church with my stepdad. I could not believe how these men were so cheery like they were getting ready to watch a movie. Instead of it being a sobering time about a personal wrong committed against the teaching of God, as I knew Him or thought I knew Him, these men, except for my father, were ready for juicy; sexy; sensual; provocative gossip as their mouths watered with ungodly anticipation. They opened the meeting with prayer and explained the reason for the meeting. Asked me, "Why do you think you are here?"

I replied, "Because I am having a baby out of wedlock." I continued by stating how I disappointed Jehovah God, my family, and myself. How remorseful I felt, and how I tried to take my life behind it all. There were no questions asked about how I tried to end my life.

Instead, the questions were, how many times did you have sex? Where were you when you had sex? How many partners have you had? Give us details of your sexual experience(s). How long did each experience last? Who was the person(s)? How long did I know him/them before having sex? How long have you been sexually active? Did you enjoy it (sex)? Asking my position(s) while in bed and in the act of sex, etc. These men were not getting answers to their questions; yet, some continued asking me like starving sex addicts. One man was punched in the side for his nonstop invasive questions and his state of curiosity. Just think, all 10 plus of them were married men, some with children, it was outrageous, to say the least. I was embarrassed enough, but there were those who wanted intimate details and I was not having it. I asked for mercy; yet, it was those elders who wanted details, so that they could go back home and tell their wives play-by-play of my sexual encounter(s). When these elders realized, I was not going to feed into their sexual fantasies, they became angry, frustrated, and confused. I knew I was not obligated to dwell on the act of fornication, only to express my sincerest repentance of not repeating the act again, outside of marriage. So, when they had decided my fate, they came back with "Disfellowship." Honestly, that was my door to what I thought of as freedom. I was okay with the verdict, but I refused to continue going to meetings and being ostracized at the same time. I felt like God was disappointed in me so what was the use of being tormented and humiliated before others?

Glory! It took me years to realize God was not angry with me and that He loved me no matter what I did or had done. You see, nothing catches God by surprise, He knows all things about us. There is nothing that can make God stop loving us.

A Valentine's Party I Will Never Forget

One evening, a couple of friends and I decided we would stop by this Valentine's party before going to the club. It was a birthday party for my friend's coworker. Once inside, this guy asked me to dance, afterward my dance, my friends were ready to leave so I said, "Good night." Going out of the door, the guy asked for my number, I gave it to him, 281-boat, or 281-coat. He thought I was pulling his leg, so I remember saying, "It's on you if you don't call it. He later shared that statement alone was enough to convince him I was being truthful. Aha. My friends and I got into the car, and guess what? I began to hum some song playing on the radio, they were shocked and so was I. Mainly, because I had not shown any sign of "life" (happiness) for months. The guy called me some days later from

New York City. I was delighted. Of course, we talked for one week on the phone before he headed back to our city. We went on a few dates, he introduced me to his family and friends, and he treated me so special. Likewise, for the very first time, I felt like a woman who carried a very precious life inside of me (my baby) and we were important. I do not have to tell you, that I no longer felt the doom and gloom, this man made me feel on top of the world and I looked forward to us spending time together. He became my friend, a person I was very comfortable around, I never felt a love like ours before. I felt secure and well-protected with him. In his arms, I felt loved, safe, and full of life. I remember, my friend and I spent the entire day together before taking me home, and about 30 minutes later I experienced labor pains.

My Emergency Delivery And Near Death Experience (March 7, 1974)

It was not long after I got home from my date that I began to have cramp-like pain that was getting worse by the minute. I told my grandmother about the pain I was experiencing and that is when she sent for the midwife in our neighborhood. She examined me and suggested they get me to the hospital, as soon as possible. When I reached the hospital, I was in so much pain, going in and out of consciousness… I was later told, that the doctors told my family if they wanted to see me alive, they needed to get there. Just before they wheeled me into labor and delivery, my friend sneaked into my room with flowers. I was so happy to see him, not knowing what I was about to face. All I knew, was this man put a joy in my heart and a song on my lips. I wanted to live again. What would follow would be truly amazing. I had a near-death experience doing delivery. I went through a tunnel so fast, I recall men, women, and children on each side of me with their hands out to welcome me, as I continued going closer and closer to the light ahead of me. Just as I was about to approach the end of the tunnel, it was on the left side that I saw family members and as I continued moving, I saw family members who were still living, and they were standing in the order of their death in the spirit. Amazingly enough, I saw my new friend standing with my family in this specific order, as well. And just before I was about to take my place in the line, I was told to "go back!" by God's voice. I, immediately, went backward out of the tunnel with enormous speed. Suddenly, I heard, "She's coming back around." When I awakened, I saw a male medical professional standing before me staring and looking very sad; yet, I was rather relieved somehow. Embarrassed, I closed my eyes and turned on my left side, to meditate on what I had just witnessed and to wrap my mind around the fact that my new male friend was going to become my husband and that he would pass on before me. Wow, that was some experience. Later, they moved me to a room with a roommate, who got to see her baby; I did not get to see my baby. I asked about my baby but was told the doctor would give more details on how "she" was doing. Interestingly, my roommate stated she heard me crying out with labor pain the night before. As she continued, she recalled my cries as scary and praying they would stop, as I could be heard throughout the unit. That alone made me even more anxious. Later, that evening I was moved to another room with an older lady, who had gallstone issues, I believe. Again, I asked questions about my baby, only to be told the doctor would talk to me in the morning. Meanwhile, that night I could hear people in the hallway as they talked saying, "Poor thing, her baby is dead," while some were laughing. I cried all night; the nurses were telling me to drink cold water because my blood pressure was up.

The next morning, the doctor came in asking, "How do you feel?"

When I said, "My baby is dead, isn't she?"

Shocked, he said, "Who told you your baby is dead?"

I said, "I heard them in the hallway talking." And that is when my roommate said,

"I heard them too, she cried all night, trying to drink cold water because her blood pressure was up."

The doctor was furious, as he stormed out of the room, he asked the nurse, "Who worked last night? Get me the names of everybody who worked last night."

I asked, "Can I see my baby? When can I see her?"

The nurse replied, "Sure, you can see her, but I have to give you something first to relax you." She later returned with a pill, and in about 45 minutes I was escorted to a room, where I got to view my baby's fingers, toes, etc. She was absolutely, beautiful, in a gorgeous outfit. Later, the doctor returned, saying, "You will have many more healthy babies." Trust me, the remainder of my hospital stay was very quiet hallways during the night and very little traffic near my door.

It was about two years later that I married my friend, just as God had revealed to me during my near-death experience. We later shared two children together, a daughter and a son. Currently, my daughter is 46 and my son is 44 years of age. I am excited to share more about my family, as my story continues.

A LIFE OF DRUGS AND ALCOHOL

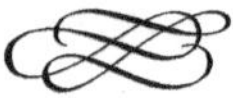

My God in heaven, after my disfellowship from the congregation of JW, I felt freedom for the first time, since my younger years. I no longer had to defend every move I made or my mistakes. Unfortunately, I was plagued with the feelings of not belonging and feeling abandoned, most of all, it was not having the love of God in my life like before. I felt I shared a remarkably close relationship with God before my fall, that is, before the condemnation in my life. Prayer, fellowshipping with God, reading His Word, and doing my best to obey his voice was my life. I remember a time of having great favor in my life, in fact, my siblings used to say, "Pearl gets whatever she wants!"

The favor of God was definitely visible in my life. I worked every summer, starting with the summer before entering the 7th grade (1967). So, from the 7th-9th grade. I worked in the office of my junior high school, except when the staff went on their vacation. That is when I worked on the campus of my local college, upon their return. Of course, from the 10th-12th grade I was very blessed to work in the State Capitol of Alabama's Treasury Dept until I decided to move to Atlanta with my friend/future husband (who was 10 years older).

Life In Atlanta

Honestly, life appeared to be wonderful for my friend and me, that is, we paid cash for whatever we wanted. Occasionally, he would surprise me with clothing purchases from major department stores and boutiques around Atlanta and then ask me to go and pick my desired style, color, and size. Oftentimes, he and I would spend our evenings together, after his hours of work as a porter for Porshe and Audi, in Atlanta's Underground. I must say, at that particular time in my life, alcohol and drugs were recreational. I worked for a few weeks in a nursing home as a certified nursing assistant (CNA), until a neighbor/co-worker reported to my job that she believed my "husband" sold drugs and I did not have to work. Needless to say, I was fired from that job after being given a polygraph test. The results concluded I did not sell drugs, but I knew someone who did. This was the result of my allowing my co-worker to see me withdraw money from my personal bank account. I cannot express how disappointed I was to lose my job. Just now, not long after she reported me to administration, trouble found her door, I learned from a friend, that she had been charged with the fatal shooting of a man and later pulling him inside the front door of her home.

Honestly, I cannot say I felt sorry for this woman at all; however, when I got the news that she would be going to prison, I paid her a visit. Of course, I did not reveal I knew it was her who went to my job administrator. According to my friend, she knew we knew all about what she was like as a person and her plans to get me fired. Likewise, during the entire visit, she looked nervous, anxious, embarrassed, and paranoid. Whenever I asked her questions about her situation her answers were short and vague; yet, the only thing that was clearly stated was her fear of sentencing. That is, going to prison for 1st-degree murder and trying to cover it up as self-defense. Ironically enough, her very own predicament stemmed from the selling of drugs, not something that she would admit to me. When I left this woman's house, I began to feel so much gratitude for my freedom. Several months later, we left Atlanta and moved to Detroit, not understanding what was taking me with me; that is, my ways, habits, and lifestyle.

Life In Detroit

My manfriend and I later moved to Detroit where I would become pregnant and we would share our wedding day with another couple, a double wedding. God was so good to me, during "labor" I did not experience any pain, the monitor allowed the medical staff to witness I was indeed in labor, and contractions were active; therefore, I was not given any anesthesia for delivery. The only pain I felt was from the sutures (stitches) and the doctor refused to anesthetize the area after I gave birth to our daughter... he just could not stand the idea I went through labor and delivery without pain. This was the opposite of my first pregnancy and delivery. The doctor was right when he stated, "You will have many more healthy babies," I thank God that all was well.

My relationship with my husband was good overall. I was not in need of anything, and my lifestyle was comfortable, especially as a stay-at-home mom. However, the older our daughter became, the more I wanted advanced job training in any area, other than the medical field. I considered cosmetology or beauty school. No matter how marvelous things may have been going for my family and me, we continued with the same habits, the same friends, and the same mindset.

Understandably, unless we change, we are going to continue getting what we always got. There was something inside of me that wanted much better and I knew that drugs and alcohol were not the answer I was seeking. Likewise, one snowstormy night I decided to leave my husband, that is, I packed my bags and traveled back to Alabama with our daughter. I remember, my daughter and I being the only passengers on the plane along with the crew, as a result, my baby and I returned home in first-class seating.

My Move Back To Home State

Upon my return home, I made a decision to pull myself up by my bootstraps and do something constructive. Likewise, about a week later I found employment with a record shop in a department store downtown. I enjoyed having something meaningful in my life. I was living life on purpose. A couple of weeks later, my husband left

Detroit and joined me and our daughter. There I was hoping a change in environment would work wonders this time. You guessed it! It did not work because we take ourselves with us wherever we go. One thing is for sure, when you keep doing what you have always done, you will continue getting what you have always gotten.

Long story short, my husband got locked up and went to prison. I was so heartbroken for me and our sweet precious daughter. Not to mention the added news of me being pregnant with our second child. The space I found myself in was overwhelming. What could I do to improve my life and the lives of my children? I knew they deserved much more than what they were living, and so did I. I wanted to be able to support them without struggling. All I could see before me was my childhood struggles coming to invade my life again. Therefore, my decision would be to enroll in cosmetology school at the local technical college.

Of course, in the meantime, visiting my husband in the county jail was the pits. Unlike my pregnancy with our first baby, I went through the pregnancy alone. I missed the love and attention I received while pregnant with our daughter. My husband was sentenced to 30 years for robbery. I cannot tell you the pain I felt in my gut. The thought of having to struggle and face lack once more in life. My solution, of course, was to go back to school for skills that would help me to provide for my growing family.

Maybe Going Back To School Would Help

What a blessing it was to enroll in cosmetology. The theory was exciting; however, the practicum aspect of the class empowered me and increased my self-esteem enormously. I studied under some of the most amazing instructors in the field. Somehow, the feelings of purpose gave me contentment. Honestly, I would be remiss if I did not tell you I smoked weed occasionally on the weekend with close friends. Although I studied hard and got good grades, I missed my husband a great deal. It was nothing like him rubbing my belly and spoiling me like he did with our firstborn daughter, Aisha. This school policy was you could only have 3 absentees per semester. I was fortunate enough to go to school up until the day of birth, Friday. Therefore, over the weekend I only missed one day of the semester. However, my occasional weekend partying resumed about three months later.

It was amazing how if I did not go around certain people I could care less about the beer and weed. A classmate of mine made it known to me that he was attracted to me. Although, I tried discouraging him by telling him I was married. He told me that did not stop a man, he included, from being attracted to me, it just made it more challenging. Regardless, I was not going to cheat on my husband. During one of our shop days for clients, this classmate was asked to do my mother's hair because I was overbooked with clients. He told my mother of his attraction to me and my disinterest in his passing, naturally, my mother was not going to okay adultery. I do not think it was so much me, but his ego as a lady's man, every week he booked very attractive women to style their hair.

Well, anyway this friend would come along before my bus arrived each morning for school when he found out my route to school. After a few rides to school, we began to smoke weed on the way to school. I cannot tell you it was a good idea for me, all it did was magnify the elephant in the room, that is, Blacks on one side and Caucasians on the other. So, one perfect day, I was assigned to clean the stock room and check out products to classmates for their clients, when one of the class bullies came for me in the stock room, that's when I motioned to grab her and she ran out screaming. No one asked me what happened, yet the police arrived putting their hands on me and asking me to leave campus. I talked with a well-respected attorney about what took place. He referred me to another attorney who asked if I wanted to return to the school. My answer was "No."

The reason I answered "no" was because I felt it was going to be nothing but chaos on my return and perhaps an even tougher time during the state board exam. It is important to note, that some months earlier, admission claimed we must pay tuition for a semester because the Pell grant would not cover it. Likewise, I borrowed the money from my grandmother and paid for it. It was a scheme to get students to quit. I knew they were targeting me because of my confidence and ability to comprehend the assignments. I could not blame anyone because I knew what I was up against and still chose to smoke weed before class. It did not matter where I went, because I always took me with me. Surely, you have recognized the patterns clearly that were in my life and the unaddressed issues that kept me spiraling down into the pit, based on my decisions.

Well, a couple of years later, I decided to go to my local university, I started out with 18 credit hours as a freshman because my class advisor thought I was an upperclassman. I kept wondering why I never got to see freshmen after 12:00 noon and my days would start at 8:00 am and end at 5:00 pm or 9:00pm some days. I made the Dean's List a couple of times and the President's List once. Likewise, my drug and alcohol use decreased tremendously. I was going every weekend to visit my husband in prison... sometimes taking my daughter on this charter bus 200 miles away for a small fee. I prepared delicious meals the day before the trip, only to borrow money from my grandparents and borrow it again. It was a vicious cycle that made me feel sorrow for myself and the life I had chosen. It was time to receive my financial assistance when the school informed me that my loans were not paid in full, and I would have to withdraw. Not so, the loans were paid from an earlier tax refund, yet, I had no documentation to prove it and no one to help me acquire it from the school, only a toll-free number that remained busy or unavailable. I want you to know I was hurt, disappointed, angry, and I felt great sorrow. This experience left me wanting to use even more, I just could not understand the things that were going on in my life, yet it all took me back to the drugs and alcohol because I did not want to feel any pain or take responsibility for my life and the disappointments in life. Something inside of me just could not give up. I had to make it by providing for my children and me, and the only way I knew would be by having a good education. Roughly, a year and a half had gone by when I decided I wanted to go back to the university and earn my bachelor's degree in psychology. I was doing fine in my studies, in fact, most of my core classes were taken in my freshmen year of college.

I Wanted A Divorce

Time moved onward and I no longer wanted to be married to my husband, I felt like life was passing me by and I was a prisoner of life. That is when I decided I would visit my husband one last time with my daughter to tell him I wanted a divorce. He would not let himself believe it, he carried on as if I just needed more time to think it through and that I still loved him. Indeed, it was true, I loved him enough to say goodbye to respect the vows and to love someone else. He, honestly, did not feel I would ever divorce him because I always stood by his side whenever he was incarcerated. I was "ole faithful Pearl," but not anymore, I wanted out of the marriage. None of his family could ever say I cheated on him. I just could not spend the time with him anymore. So, he received a "Dear John" (John was indeed his name) letter from me with the papers asking for my divorce and the use of my maiden name. I cut off all ties to him, meaning, no more letters; visits; or phone calls. He was not a happy person at all. I received the divorce, and his signature was not needed for the divorce to be granted to me (May 1979).

A year and some months later, I found it difficult to get up for an 8:00 class, only to find out that I was pregnant with my third child. Oh my, more visible patterns were present. Think about it, the drugs and alcohol were a part of my lifestyle, and anytime I made the decision to go to school, I would later find out that I was pregnant; apart from my first live birth (daughter born in Detroit). At this particular time in my life, I decided to take the Air Force exam; only to find out later, that I passed, and my husband hid my enlistment papers that were mailed out to me. I remember getting 200% on the Air Force exam taken, after my high school graduation, as well. Interestingly, at that time in 1974, I needed to gain 15 lbs. before I could enlist...it did not happen. Nevertheless, I always found myself fighting for something and not achieving goals like I did when I was in God's perfect will for my life. This was my biggest struggle, as the drugs and the alcohol continued. In 1981, my daughter, Shimere, was born. I remember, my grandfather telling me, "Every time I turn on a light in the house you turn on a light."

I knew I had a place to come to if I ever needed it. No questions would be asked. My children were safe because my family did not want anyone outside of our immediate family babysitting them. This arrangement was fine with me. The time had come when I wanted to live on my own and enjoy everything that that entailed.

On My Own

I was able to get an apartment right after my divorce was final. During the school year, my oldest two children and niece lived with me during the weekdays and at my grandparents' house every weekend, faithfully. My granddaddy would pick them up like clockwork after work every Friday and bring them back Sunday evening with money for them and me. God knows, I believe I stayed in addiction as long as I did because I had enablers… people I could get money from freely. I saw an opportunity to attend a vocational training school to become a Certified Nursing Assistant (CNA). I graduated top of my class and was later hired at the facility where I completed my training.

In fact, about 5 years later, I lost my apartment after working and not reporting the increase to the landlord. This was another unwise decision. Therefore, to settle the bill, I needed quite a bit of money before the deadline. Honestly, I found myself unwilling to rectify the problem with the landlord responsible, for keeping my apartment. So, I decided to run back to my grandparent's house for cover, back to living for a minimal/free amount. Every place I went, I took me with me. Likewise, there wasn't any difference when I got a ticket for DUI (driving under the influence). I was given a fine by the court and told to attend DUI school. During the time of this class, my classmates and I were told never to attend classes drunk and I did not. I smoked weed and drank earlier in the day before class and after class. During the last night of class, our "graduation," we had a guest speaker. This man poured out his heart about how he was a repeat offender (several DUIs), and how his addiction to alcohol caused him to take the life of a woman and her unborn child. Believe me, there was not a dry eye in the place.

I must say, after that, I never got behind the wheel of a car while drinking alcohol again… so, I decided to walk while drinking, that is, from my home to the club and/or vice versa. Interestingly, I thought I was committing the lesser of the two crimes by walking and not driving. However, if stopped by the police while walking drunk, it is called public intoxication. I never wanted to address the real issue, Me! There was underlined hurt and pain that would eventually force me to look at myself, whenever the pain outweighed the pleasure.

I Moved Back To My Grand-Parent's Home

I returned to my grandparents' home. It was at that time, that I decided I wanted to further my knowledge of nursing and become a Licensed Practical Nursing (LPN). My love for people and a genuine desire to see them happy and healthy is one of my passions. I discovered this love for the medical field during my

11th and 12th years of high school in Health Occupations Classes.

Nursing classes were going very well. I was so very proud of myself. I helped the children with their assignments in the afternoon and prepared them for school the following day. I grocery shopped and took the children to doctor/dental appointments and school activities.

Again, I could see myself winning by being a responsible and productive adult. My, my! Just how long would it be before the alcohol/drugs claimed more areas of my life to destroy, hinder, steal, and delay?!

I Could Run But I Could Not Hide

Just now, I was determined to turn my situation around by going to nursing school to become a licensed nurse. I refused to be held down any longer. I was going to beat the terrible hand I had been dealt, not wanting to face my addiction, no matter how many times it appeared in the equation. No matter where I went or what I decided to do, I was always taking me with me. The insanity of doing the same thing repeatedly, yet, expecting different results.

Interestingly, nursing school was fantastic. I began to build self-esteem and self-worth began to surface. I wanted so much to care for my three children properly without having to depend so much on my grandparents and mother. My family supported me with encouraging words and loving deeds for the children and myself.

Somewhere around my third quarter of school, I felt I had this monster covered. The disease of addiction will wait for you, that is, I smoked weed and drank alcohol when things were good, bad, or indifferent. I literally celebrated you, me, and everyone else, regardless of the circumstances. If someone died, a baby was born, etc. it just did not matter the occasion, every occasion was party time. I recalled looking for someone who could be a sure drinking and smoking partner. Aha, I did not have to look far, he served in the school cafeteria. I, purposely, went after him for what I called benefits and won. I knew my classmates were wondering, why him? It was indeed intentional; although it wasn't much they could say because some of us would go to lunch and afterward smoke weed. One of my classmates kept a coffee cup, not sure what that was all about... I had my suspicions. The guy I chose to be my "get high" partner, picked me up each morning and took me home. Of course, we spent plenty of evenings smoking and drinking after school. God knows, I really could not tell him why I came after him. Perhaps, he had a good idea. I must admit feelings came into play. I have recovering friends who would say, "When two people lie down together, one of them is going to get up with some feelings."

Believe me, after some time I developed feelings for this person. Keep in mind, my real lover was the addiction. It did not take long for me to go deeper into self-centeredness, selfishness, pride, entitlement, and more. In my last quarter as a nursing senior, I maintained an A average.

I was proud of that and the fact that our class started with forty-something students, about 12 passed finals, and 7 passed the state board exam. I passed the state board exam and was later offered a job as I and others waited for our license to come in the mail. The relationship would soon end because the guy I was dating started to feel some type of way. Not to mention, his class was a two-year program as he related to me... I truly never knew if this was so or not. All I know, I started to make great money, and things were coming together for me and the children. The money magnified the addiction even more, that is, more weed more alcohol. During this time, I applied for employment at another medical facility and made top pay as a skilled nurse in a skilled patient care unit.

Two years had passed and time for my license renewal. On the application, a question asked if I had been arrested in the last two years. Oh, my how I agonized over that question. I was afraid if I answered no, something would come up on the unit, in which staff and I would be investigated. I just did not want to take that risk. I also thought that if I lied about the arrest, I could easily lie about giving a patient their medication. Well, little did I know I was being convicted for the bad choices that I made in my life. So, after about a week passed, I decided to tell the truth by answering yes to a prior arrest.

My application was flagged and had to go before the board of nursing. I was placed on probation for one year, which in turn allowed me to work with stipulations. For instance, attending an addiction program for one year and working directly under an assigned RN to monitor my performance, I was allowed to pass out medicines, as well. Likewise, because of the prideful person I had become, I did not realize the extended help I would receive. In the interview with the state board, they asked me why I told the truth, with so many applicants for renewal... I could have easier gotten away. That is, when I told them lying would have made it easier to lie about my patients and their care.

Honestly, it had to be God. I understand now, that it was The Holy Spirit that convicted me and showed me I needed help. That is, I was out of control. Pride would not allow me to be grateful for the opportunity to work and get help for the addiction. Therefore, I went into a deep depression and decided to advance in my drug usage with something I had never been interested in before. It was "crack cocaine." Crack kept me out there longer than I wanted to be before surrendering my will over to God.

THE BEGINNING OF MY EIGHT YEARS NIGHTMARE

Yes, you heard me correctly, crack cocaine kept me in denial and in addiction longer than I was able to handle along with the alcohol, weed, cigarettes, and behaviors. What started out as experimentation, later recreational, had its claws in me and I did not know how to shake it. I was changing more and more. There were times I would read my bible or biblical literature to check my thinking, sort of gauging where I was mentally. All I knew was that I needed God to work in my life, but I had yet to surrender. I wanted to learn how to use drugs successfully. Clearly, that was not going to happen.

There were stories upon stories of what I experienced using drugs that would probably make you think, "Surely this will make her stop," but it did not. I recalled one of my high buddies and I going to buy drugs in the neighborhood. While there, I began to feel uneasy.

Something was not right; I could not enjoy the high. So, my friend and I left. No sooner than he and I got on the sidewalk in front of the house, who do you think showed up? We called them "21 Jump Street," those police officers riding in and standing outside the trucks with weapons ready to draw. We were grateful we were not a part of that drug bust for sure. I remember having police officers call me by my name in certain neighborhoods. I can remember police officers driving by saying, "Don't go back there," after I had left a party. Many, many times it was God saving my life, like the time I would stay over this guy's house from time to time.

Some days, when I was off work, I would stay at this boarding house until he returned from work. However, during the day most of the boarders would be at work or someplace, except for the boarder upstairs next door to my friend's room. When I was there during the day and had to leave to get ready for work, I noticed he always had a lot of company. So, I began to think, what if this man makes someone angry, they could easily hurt him and shoot through the walls at me.

Interestingly, I thought to myself, there is no way that they would harm him and not harm me, even if they had to break the weak doors down in that old historic house. So, I prayed that no harm would come to me in that house. Almighty God heard my prayers because not long after that, some of the boarders and several other people were found murdered in that house.

When I tell you, I praised God for sparing my life, I am not kidding you. There was always something about me praising God… I would walk and talk to God while going to buy or use drugs. Talking about God with others while getting high was not unusual for me. I understood where two or three were gathered talking about God, he was in our midst. We were protected from further harm. This is my experience, believe me, my spirituality was zero; but, I knew I could not afford to be without God in my life even in my sinning and disobedience. I knew I needed God's hand and I was not going to turn his hand loose, completely.

Addiction is so cunning and baffling, it made me think for years I was not so bad, that I could still be a good mom and productive individual. When I spiraled down into the pit without a job, the disease of addiction told me it was ok. Especially, since my grandfather had already proclaimed my children and I would always have a home. It was true what Granddaddy was saying, but I bought into the lie, that I did not have to do anything to get out of that pit of addiction.

My Grandmother's Death

My God, my grandmother's passing could not stop me from using; although, I know I was summoned in the spirit to go home and check on my grandmother. On that particular day, I was at a boarding house and while I was sitting outside, I decided to call my mother to pick me up to go home. When I got there, my grandmother said she was not feeling well. I remember telling her if she was not better in the morning, I would take her to the doctor. She told me, "I'm alright now." I reassured her I would check on her in the morning and I said, "Good Night."

The next morning, I woke up feeling like something was not right. One of my children's cousins would drop off her son each weekday day morning before going to work. We loved that baby. He was probably about 6 months old at the time. My grandmother had grown very fond of him and looked forward to his arrival each day. Interestingly, on that morning, I could tell he wanted to see her. He kept looking at the door to the bedroom and trying to get off the bed to go see her. My God! Fear gripped me. I was too afraid to go to her bedroom. I began to ponder, exactly, what did she mean last night when she said, "I'm alright now?" Suddenly, I could hear my aunt calling my grandmother, "Madear," she shouted. I ran to see what was happening.

My grandmother had gotten out of bed and tried dressing herself when she collapsed onto the floor. I called the ambulance and called my mother. The medics arrived and got her on the stretcher and into the ambulance, where they tried resuscitation before driving to the hospital without a siren. My mother and I followed. When we arrived at the hospital, we were told my grandmother had passed on. It was difficult seeing my mother crying for her mother, while I tried to make sense of it all. Again, God got me home, out of the street to see my praying grandmother alive for the last time.

Still, it was not enough to stop me from using alcohol and drugs. I told myself, this was reason enough to use even more, my encourager was gone, and I had let her down. The alcohol and drug use continued without any shame or excuses because I felt in control, after all, I could stop anytime I got tired of myself. I just wasn't sick and tired of me.

Please, Don't Lock Up My Son

The progression of the disease of addiction was cunning. I could not see the effect that it had on my children. Nor the influence other adults had on my children as a result of me not being an active parent in those critical teenage years. The thought of me using drugs and alcohol when my children, undoubtedly, had to make tough decisions on their own because of my selfishness. Of course, this led me to identify a resilience in my children that was in operation. However, that was not enough for my son. Truthfully, without getting too deeply into the case because of the expectation of future vindication, I will lay down a foundation of innocence. A robbery that ended in murder took place in the neighborhood. Several young teens and my son were charged with the offense. My son was said to be guilty by association, that is, being placed at the crime scene during its occurrence. Likewise, in his defense, he testified in detail what occurred and offered all his clothing for the forensic lab… **no trace of blood was found on** his clothes, socks, or sneakers. It was obvious he **was not** present during the murder.

Of course, as a mother on drugs and alcohol, I was not helping my son's case at all. During this particular time, mothers were losing their teen sons to death for their cars, and sneakers, and being set up by teen girls in luring them to their houses for jealous teen boys. So many lives were lost, especially, young males and foolish rivalries. Honestly, I felt helpless toward my son; yet, I was grateful to God he was alive. My 17-year-old was sentenced to life without parole in 1995, to date he has done 28 years in prison. Since then, he has received his GED, earned college credits, married/separated, and drawing closer to God and purpose. We understand Jehovah God doesn't make mistakes; therefore, my son is waiting on Jehovah to vindicate his name and get all of the Glory for his life story.

My Ex-Husband's Return Home Ended Tragically

My ex-husband was released from prison, of course, that meant he was very active in our two children's lives. This included spending time with our daughter, who was pregnant with our first grandchild. He even went so far as to invite her to live with him, while he helped her to get her first apartment. My son entered prison during the incarceration of his father at 17 years old. Sentenced to life in prison with the possibility of parole for a crime that took place while he was held under gunpoint (duress) for robbery and another crime of murder that followed without his presence. My son has been incarcerated for 25+ years to this date. I have faith that Almighty God's will in His timing will vindicate my son's name and restore him, as God has promised.

After my ex-husband was released from prison, he and

our daughter traveled many miles to visit our son. I was so caught up in my addiction that I could not settle my differences with their father long enough to ride in the car to see my son. Drugs made me selfish and self-centered. One particular visiting day, my ex-husband came to pick up our daughter from the house. After they left, I cried uncontrollably. I did not understand why I was crying so deeply, with such great sadness. The next week, their dad called and asked how I was doing. It was after all of that crying, that I was able to be civil with him before calling my daughter to the phone. That same week leading up to the weekend, my daughter was talking to her father on the phone, when someone knocked on his door. My daughter said she heard him ask, "Who is it?"

However, she was unable to hear the reply. My ex-husband returned the phone and said he would call our daughter back and they hung up. In less than an hour someone was calling my daughter to say her father had been shot and killed. Oh my, when she told me, I understood why I cried like I was moaning about the death of a loved one, but most of all, we ended up as friends.

Needless to say, my ex-husband's death shook me to my core, about three months later I found myself asking for help for the addiction that plagued my life for years. I received that help from an anonymous 12 Steps and

12 Traditions Program. There were men and women who taught me to surrender to that new way of life without the use of drugs and alcohol; they taught me to trust the God of my understanding and to allow Him to fill that void of much-depleted spirituality. I truly needed the program because I felt I failed and disappointed God, my family, and myself. Today, I am looking forward to celebrating 25 years on July 18, 2023.

More importantly, I remembered the near-death experience I had in the delivery room, in the early days of my ex-husband and I dating. In the near-death experience, I saw my family members lined up in the order of their death and my ex-husband was standing among them (not married at the time). This gave me knowledge that this man would become my husband and he would pass before me. I will go into more detail about this near-death experience in another chapter covering some of the heavenly and divine encounters I have experienced over the years.

FINDING MY WAY BACK TO GOD

My God, I am so grateful for the 12 Steps Program and the members who were available when I arrived. The moment I realized I could not stay stopped from drugs and alcohol, something clicked in my head. I was surrounded by folks who knew the hopelessness I faced. They understood using against my will. Said to myself I would not use the hard drugs, but substitute them for a drink of alcohol, not understanding alcohol is a drug, as well. Smoking crack took me to another level of getting high because it is the greatest liar. Cocaine told me I did not have a problem, and that I could quit anytime I wanted. It was not true. However, the more time that went by in the program with a loving and caring sponsor (a mentor that guides you through the program on one from their experiences) the more I could see God forgiving me and wanting the best for me. I was able to understand that humility, surrendering, and acknowledging I could not do it alone without a power greater than drugs. I called that power God. I saw my life change before my eyes for the better. Things I took pride in before the drugs began to look attractive again, for instance, I have always had a love for fashion. My conservative way of dressing inspired me, not too trendy but a comfortable middle ground of modest dressing. I loved learning, which entailed plenty of how-to-readings, going to school for advancement, holding down a promising job, going to a house of worship, having a serious prayer life, and frequently reading my Bible. All of these activities put me back on the road to sanity and almighty God, Jehovah. As a matter of fact, let me tell you what happened when I got clean.

I got my first job after 28 days of being clean and serene, as an associate in the seafood department of a well-known grocery store chain. Of course, after about 6 months I became a seafood manager. The work was challenging, but it was rewarding at the same time while living drug-free. I would say at about the 2-year mark of being clean and sober, the job of manager demanded more of me from the store managers. That is, pressure to increase sales; order and display inventory; plan associates' work schedules, etc. One thing that was taught in the program was H.A.L.T. Never get too hungry, angry, lonely, or tired... those are the enemies of recovery. My job as a seafood manager was getting more and more overwhelming, no matter what I did to make it successful in the eyes of the senior managers it just was not good enough. Therefore, I decided to give my store managers two weeks' notice, because I refused to fall prey to drugs again. No job meant enough to take me back to where I was delivered. All of the talk to convince me to stay as seafood manager fell on deaf ears, especially when I learned my bonuses were given to a former manager and who knows who else. Considering, I served under two department managers before I became a manager.

Working in the Prison System

I will never forget how I landed this honorable position with the prison system; I was about two years clean and sober when I decided to go to a job fair with my granddaughter. I cannot tell you my expectations were high because they were not. I was really trying to make certain that my granddaughter had transportation to get there, and I was going along for the ride. In fact, when we were leaving the car, I decided to leave my resume in the car, not thinking there would be a company present that could use my prior medical experience. Fortunately, I was wrong. There was a company that would consider me as a nursing assistant at a local prison. Therefore, I informed the representative that my resume was in my car due to my low expectations of finding a good fix. Honestly, I believe, initially, she thought I was pulling her leg about my resume being in the car. Nevertheless, she was pleasantly surprised or relieved when I returned with my impressive resume. I was called for an interview immediately. I cannot tell you how grateful I was to get a shot at this new position. During my interview I was asked about the long pause in my work history, that is when I mentioned my struggle with drugs and alcohol; yet, I had been clean and sober for 2 years at the time of the interview. Amazingly, to my surprise, the interviewer thanked me for my honesty and shared a similar experience. Do you mind if I tell you I was hired on the spot with a friendly tour of the facility with great introductions of health care staff, as well as, the staff of correctional officers? Yes indeed, I was so thrilled and proud of myself for not being ashamed of my past.

Interestingly, my duties as a nursing assistant took me back to my first love, health occupations. All the wonderful thoughts of why I became a nurse in the first place flooded my mind and heart. I was back in my element, my God-given talent of serving others. My duties included but were not limited to new admissions, routine vital signs, infirmary (hospital), sick calls (inmates' doctor's appointment), Department of Corrections (DOC) incoming and outgoing transfers/assessments, (DOC) body charts (injuries), emergencies, infirmary log of inmates (count), dental sick call vital signs, filing and pulling medical charts, assist LPNs/RNs with medical procedures, calling physician in case of emergency with vital signs for instructions to relate to emergency nurse, copying charts in cases of death, notifying DOC staff of emergency transfers with documentation, vital signs for those applying for medical/corrections positions, etc. Glory to God… this was a great fit!

My Heart for the Inmates Increased

Oh, my God! It is amazing to me how a person's heart can soften when they are shown authentic caring and support. Although I was not a softie, the inmates knew I sincerely cared for them and would not allow them to suffer in their bodies if I could help them. Whenever they were in pain or needed to sign up for sick calls, they would purposefully ask for Ms. Rivers. Of course, not only was it my job, but I was good at making sure pain management was available. I remember working a particular weekend when many of the regular nurses were off duty. During this time I worked with new employees who were not as familiar with protocol as myself; therefore, when the nurse was about to send an inmate back to his bunk with a toothache until Monday… I just had to tell her, "Oh no, we do not allow them to suffer, especially, not with a toothache. He can have something for pain until he is seen by the dentist on Monday." My God, if you have ever suffered toothache pain, you know how thankful that inmate was for my insight. Over time, it was just the little things of showing mercy that developed my ability to care even more deeply, after all. You see, I have a son in the prison system, as well. Therefore, I can assure you that I would want someone to have mercy on my loved ones, no matter what that need may have been or is.

There were so many cancer patients on the ward who were treated by our nursing facility. In fact, our facility received so many inmates from all over the State of Alabama, that you would have thought we were a specialty unit for inmates with cancer. Naturally, seeing inmates going through the process of fighting this disease, there were many who fought back and won; likewise, there were those inmates who were overpowered by the disease and did not survive its deadly sting for one reason or another. It was the policy of the facility (medical/officers' staff) to remove the inmate from the hospital ward and place him into a private cell on the ward, whenever this inmate was facing his final days of life. This gesture was to allow the individual the privacy to expire with dignity and respect, as well as, giving the other patients the opportunity and space to grief in their own special way. The moral of the patient is important in their healing process.

Sharing My Recovery from Drugs and Alcohol In The Prison

Knowledge of my recovery from drugs and alcohol came about with me sharing openly about the struggles I've faced in life, and how it could all be turned around with a renewed and willing mind to change for the good. Over the years, there were many conversations that I shared with inmates about making a change and wanting more for themselves and loved ones. It was through one of those conversations, that a mental health counselor heard me encouraging several inmates, and asked me to speak to one of his group sessions. I did this upon his request and my scheduler as a nursing assistant. Of course, I enjoyed those 45-minute group sessions, they eventually got me an invitation to speak with the inmates in the population. These were inmates interested in participating in a 1hour substance abuse meeting per week per DOC (The Department of Corrections). The turnouts were amazing and so were our thought-provoking topics on the subject of substance abuse, recovery, and prevention.

My Special Time Of Prayer With The Brass And Others

I remember a woman of faith sharing with me how important she felt it would be to pray corporately at the start of our morning shift. This would be for all individuals interested and free to participate Mondays-Fridays. I felt it was an excellent idea and so I joined without any hesitation. I think it was about a week in progress when The Captain at Kilby and several other officers joined us, faithfully, each morning. In fact, these individuals were still praying faithfully every Monday-Friday, when I decided to leave the facility and apply for a new position at another facility. There will be more about this in the next topic, for sure. Likewise, our Captain was a believer and one of faith, praise, testimony, and worship. I must tell you, when we had prayer, we had church! I loved it because I felt covered by God, and I knew he was present. The best part was we agreed, and The Captain and Warden agreed to pray, as well. I cannot express the goodness and gratitude I felt being a part of those who sought God early for his love, wisdom, protection, understanding, and application. It made such an incredible impact on me to witness how God's children can be found in every arena, it is up to us to make ourselves known.

Nursing License Returned

Wow, wow, wow! I got my nursing license reinstated after many stipulations, challenges, and plain old hatefulness, jealousy, and ungodliness. Remember, I told you how strong our prayers were in the mornings, right? Well, the enemy was in for a losing battle. I knew we had the victory, and we had more than enough to send the devil packing. It was at this time even more evil was rearing its ugly head and being exposed. I became extremely sensitive to the spirit. I remember one day telling the medical doctor how my co-workers helped me by taking part in notarized paperwork concerning my character, skills, goals, behavior, etc. They played a big part in my reinstatement as an LPN (Licensed Practical Nurse) under their supervision as RNs (Registered Nurses) and LPNs. I also mentioned to him that the last step of the reinstatement process was for me to include a fee (around $800.00) and if he would be interested in contributing to the cause. He commended me for my progress and effort and that was the end of our conversation. One other thing, I mentioned to him I had a fast-approaching deadline and any donation he would like to contribute would be greatly appreciated. Lo and behold, the next morning I got to work, there was a plain envelope filled with cash addressed to me. I was totally overjoyed and in incredible shock, as well, asking who my contributor was… no one claimed the blessing bestowed upon me, not even the doctor. It was totally anonymous! What I call an incredible God-answered prayer. So excited I was told by the Captain to secure the money for my car. I returned to the facility praising God because I was now closer to having my license placed in my hands in a matter of days. I received my contract and was looking forward to working in my present facility (the prison). However, when it was time to sign my contract, I could not believe the Director of Nursing Staff denied me employment as a professional while trying her best to help an individual get instated with zero days clean (she alerted me she used over the weekend and she felt horrible). I, on the other hand, had maintained being clean and sober for 6.5 years, in 2005 (less than 2 months away from celebrating 7 years of being clean and sober). All I knew was I had to find a place of employment for my upgraded position, I did not want to waste any time in walking into my dream come true. I was blessed to return to my former place of employment. I worked for about 1.5 months before I was bitten by something that made my right ankle swell 4 times its normal size. After about 2 days I was not able to get out of bed without excruciating pain. What was going on, my whole body was hurting day and night non-stop? I could not attempt to walk to the bathroom without tears and pain. Nevertheless, it goes without saying, that I was unable to fulfill my nursing career because of my inability to walk and the severe pain in my body, especially, in my hands. It should be noted that in 4 months, I was awarded Social Security Disability. More on the challenges I faced in an upcoming chapter, stay with me, okay?

My Mother's Death

Oh, my! When I think about the time my mother came to me and said, "I have already told your sisters and brothers, if something happens to me to the point, I don't know who I am or I am being kept alive by a machine, let me go." She continued, "I would like to die with dignity and respect."

I remember replying to her by saying, "Momma, you know, I would not allow you to suffer or have a low quality of life." I assured her that she could depend on me. Especially, as someone with an understanding of the medical profession. Immediately, I could see the relief in her eyes as her request was made known and accepted. My mother was my greatest friend, supporter, and motivator, therefore, the thought of her being on the go and enjoying friends and family made me truly admire her. As for myself, on the contrary, I could hardly put one foot before the other without the assistance of a walker or cane. Honestly, a walker was safer and steadier for me because I lacked much strength in my body to stand firmly. There was a time when I needed to leave the house for business, my mother helped me to her car. Literally, quite weak, I tried opening the car door without any success, my mother came to my aid as she bumped the car door against me… making me stumble backward, only to catch me and lower me into the car as she bumped my head. (Lolol). All I could hear her saying with each bump was, "Ooooh, sorry sorry, Pearl, I am sooo sorry." I know, she wanted to laugh, but I was so put off by it, she held her laugh for later (out of my presence, lol). Just an idea of how close we were as mother and daughter.

If there was anything my mother enjoyed more than prayer and God's Presence, it was studying her bible and witnessing to others. I will not forget the time something happened, and my mother left her bible at the Kingdom Hall (church). Someone called and said they had it and would get it to my mother that day (Sunday). Well, I was over to her house and several hours had passed, still no bible. I could tell my mother was frustrated because her bible was her lifeline to God. I asked, when were they bringing her bible, and she replied, "If I had known it was going to be this long, I would have told them, I will pick it (bible) up myself!" My mother felt as though her bible was being held, hostage.

My mom and I were going someplace, and I mentioned the Thanksgiving plans I had for family dinner. According to my journal, it was during the end of October. I was trying to get some feedback from my mother; however, looking back, she seemed distanced and sad in her thoughts and demeanor about Thanksgiving. I could tell she did not want to discuss it at that time. Although, I was excited and looking forward to feasting with my loved ones. Interestingly, about a week later, on Sunday, November 4, 2007, my mother went to the Kingdom Hall and collapsed after the services. My brother was present when they called for emergency assistance for my mother. Likewise, my brother called and said my mother had been admitted to the hospital for a stroke. My God! I felt helpless and numb. It was so unbelievable what I was hearing about my momma. My queen, the love of my life, my covering (physically and spiritually). It was reported by doctors that my mother had 2 blood clots in her brain. The local hospital staff felt it was imperative that my mother be transferred to Birmingham (UAB) for advance treatment on Monday, November 5... I cried out to Jehovah that his will be done for my mother. Unable to visit her I relied on the report of others, which made me feel even more helpless. That's when I requested the contact information of the medical doctors. Likewise, after talking to one of the attending physicians I decided I must get to the hospital right away. Moreover, my youngest daughter told me, during her visit that day, which was Monday, that when she told my mother, "Pearl, my momma loves you." At that moment, my daughter recalled, my mother moved her hands and tried to speak. I was convinced I had to get there immediately. I planned to go to the hospital with my brother on his next visit to the hospital. Seeking Jehovah for His Will and not mine, I cried out to Jehovah for wisdom, selflessness, understanding, and application. We were able to go back Thursday, my brother, daughter, niece, and granddaughter accompanied me. They also assisted with my mobility by providing a transport chair. When I arrived at the unit, I visited my mother to get a clear understanding of her condition and potential needs. I noticed she was in great pain, and I saw the white ring in her eyes. The medication was not helping her. I realized my mother's request not suffering and her quality of life was before me. I talked with her team and nursing staff about the medication, her quality of life, and her right to expire with dignity and respect. My mother's lips were swollen, and I am not sure why; however, after talking with the medical team, my decision to move her to Palliative Care immediately was carried out. Thank you, Holy Spirit for directing me in the management of my mother's comfort and quality of life. My siblings started to arrive in the unit, including my two out-of-state sisters. My mother held on to hear all of our messages. My message to her was I will continue to be a good mother to my children and grandchildren, I will stay clean and serene till death, and I will live life the way I have been taught, that is, a life pleasing to Jehovah.

Monday, November 19, 2007, around 5:15 am I received a phone call from my sister stating my momma just transition. Honestly, hearing this news I was saddened, yet I was happily relieved. No more suffering my dear sweet loving kind momma. Jesus Jesus Jesus! Thanksgiving was in four days, of course, I recalled trying to talk to my mom about my dinner plans for our family and she looked so sad and broken. My God, Jehovah! She knew she would no longer be here with us.

Friday, November 23, 2007, today after Thanksgiving, we buried my mother. I could feel the presence of Jehovah, angels, and the spirit of my momma in the sanctuary. The presence was so strong and heavy as I continued to walk closer to the lying state of my mother's shell. I automatedly held my head down in honor of my mother's life because of the undeniable weight upon me. And with strength, my head was held high as my nephew escorted me to my seat as requested. I walked with a cane, yet, I barely had enough to stand. Likewise, standing and viewing my mother was not an option for me. Therefore, I viewed my mother's remains one last time from my seat. I felt the heaviness of each of my siblings as they entered and were seated. Tears rolled down the cheeks of two of my brothers. When the service was over, I was reminded of the painful standing I must endure as I reached for my cane. I felt all eyes on me, as my nephew and I prepared to walk that lonely aisle that my mother walked so many times up until now. My, My! The pain in my knees and sorrow in my heart overwhelmed me. It is very important to note, that I witnessed a peace that surpassed all understanding. I honored, loved, respected, and appreciated my mother. I am thankful to Almighty God for my mother, Annie Lee (Rivers) Lee, and everything it took to align me with God's Perfect Will. I Shall Always Love My Momma!

My Return To The House Of Worship

Glory to God! I had no idea that three years of my life would mostly be confined to a bed. However, in those 3 years, I would draw closer to God and make time to finish my bachelor's degree online. Through it all, I made a promise to God, that if He would get me out of that bed and allow me to walk, I would walk to the nearest church. I was pleasantly surprised when one Sunday my oldest daughter and her three children attended a church about 3 blocks away from our home where an intersection of West (home) and East (church) met. She and the children returned happily telling me how friendly everyone was, how they greeted all first-time visitors, that visitors were greeted by Senior Pastors, and given a gift of appreciation. It happens, that the gift was a CD of a sermon preached by the Senior Pastor. I genuinely enjoyed it, so much so, that I decided the next Sunday, I would walk to church with my walker! My daughter offered to give me a ride, but I refused because I said, I promised to walk, first! Yes, Lord! I made it there and was blessed with a ride back home. Praise and Worship was amazing, I have not stopped since that day on October 26, 2008. The next Sunday, the church van picked me up and carried me back to church. That Sunday, I decided to walk with my cane. I was progressing along, and I loved giving God all of the Glory. Amazingly enough, it became official on November 9, 2008, when I joined the church. I was extremely excited to worship and hear the word of God for my life and my loved ones. Of course, not only was this Sunday special because I joined the church but also, because I decided to put the cane down and walk on my own. Over the years of being a faithful member I would receive more healing; receive godly directions and instructions; attend new members, discipleship, leadership, intercessors/prophetic, dreams/visions, deliverance, healing room classes; Care Ministry; Prophetic Team Member; Women Fellowship; and Women in Ministry International (WIMI). I am so grateful to God for what He has done in my life. Sending me back in his presence, that is, to a House of Worship that He had chosen for my spiritual, physical, mental, emotional, and financial growth. Now, I would like to go just a little deeper into what my relationship has been with God in the supernatural. That is, I would like to share several of my encounters with heaven in this next chapter. Are you ready? Hopefully, you are ready for take-off.

MY ENCOUNTERS WITH HEAVEN
AND HELL

If you recall, in Chapter 1 I mentioned having a near-death experience while giving birth to a baby girl. Meaning, I went into the hospital on March 6, 1974, and that was when I experienced my first Heavenly Encounter. I hid my pregnancy for months from my family and the church elders (Jehovah's Witnesses), therefore, I was not receiving the prenatal care I needed after finding out I was pregnant about 3 months earlier. Which means, that any vitamins, tests, or procedures I may have needed were not done. Of course, that alone was putting the baby's and my life in danger. Today, I realized just how foolish and dangerous that was. Remembering back on that day, I had gone out on my third or fourth date with the young man I met at Valentine's party, the one that made my heart and me sing again, literally. I had been home for about 30 minutes from my date, when all of a sudden my stomach began to cramp, and my back began to hurt. I told my grandmother about the pain I was having when she inquired again how far along, I was. When I told her I was in my eighth month, she appeared to be overly concerned. She immediately got in touch with the midwife in our neighborhood to check on me. After checking me, the midwife told my grandmother to get me to the hospital immediately. After being rushed to the hospital and placed in a room, I heard my "friend" say, "How are you?" When I looked to answer him, I noticed the lovely flowers in his hands… I remember asking him, "How did you get in?"

He snuck in and snuck out quietly. It was strange, now that I recall, a nurse asked me where the flowers came from and how they got into my room. Honestly, answering her question was not at the top of my list.

In the meantime, I was so heavily sedative, that I do not remember the actual birthing experience. In fact, I later learned the doctors were telling my family to get everyone to the hospital, immediately, if they wanted to see me alive for the last time. However, the next day I was told by a patient in bed B that my screaming could be heard all over the hospital, as well as my crying out for help. I later learned I had been diagnosed with pre-eclampsia, which caused me to have extremely high blood pressure, which in turn put my unborn baby and me in extreme danger of losing our lives. This in turn explained why the doctors were telling my family to get everyone to the hospital, in order, to see me for the last time.

My First Heavenly Encounter

Clearly, it was somewhere in this time frame I died and entered a tunnel while I traveled swiftly toward the light at the end of the tunnel. There were people on my left and right of the tunnel in a single file line greeting me with their hands extended, smiling as they welcomed me. I was passing by them at great speed. As I passed them, I noticed their clothing and realized whatever garments they were last seen in on earth were what they had on in Heaven, for instance, some were in suits, dresses, shorts, tops, pants, etc. and they were giving off an incredible glow along with the brilliant light at the end of the tunnel that I was traveling towards. Of course, just as I was getting to the end of the tunnel, I looked to the left and saw my family members. Remarkably, they were standing in the order of their deaths, for some, it was a future death. Even more interesting, I saw my newfound lover standing among family members who had not passed on yet, such as my paternal and maternal grandparents; uncles;

aunts; cousins; etc... And to think that my maternal grandmother was holding my newborn daughter. Just as I was getting ready to take my place in line, God said, "Go back, it's not time." So, I went out of the tunnel backward with great speed and strong suctioning power. That experience told me quite a bit, that is, my baby died; my new friend was going to be my husband, and he would pass after my maternal grandmother, before my maternal grandfather, mother, and uncle... all at the end of the line. Just know, I was never the same after that encounter.

Because of this encounter, I learned of God's love for me and that He was not angry with me no matter what anyone or any religious group said or felt. After that, I just wanted nothing to do with Jehovah's Witnesses (JW's). How could they claim to be the "right and only true religion" of Almighty God and turn their backs on me... just because they had the power in their hands to do so? All my life, to that point, JW's were all I had as a representation of God. I was willing to end my life and the life of my baby, that is, to go to hell, because I thought I disappointed my God and he did not love me anymore, only to find out, that that religion was entirely wrong for me and they had changed and watered down the bible so much, it was extremely difficult for me to know and recognize the true promises of God.

My January 2000 Encounter

During this time, I worked 7-3 shift unless I was working a double. That day, there was a pull on me to hurry and get ready for bed. Finally, I took my shower and got ready for bed. As soon as my head hit the pillow, I was asleep. Right away, I was greeted by my angel, who told me, "You have a divine appointment with The Lord!"

Immediately, he and I were getting into this contraption that looked like a royal stagecoach without the horses or driver that reminded me of a ski lift in the air without the cable. It was extremely fast and beautiful. We passed beautiful mountains and arrived quickly in a golden city. This beautiful lift stopped in this lovely area where everyone arrived and jumped off their lift quickly. People were arriving continually. We could see God's Throne raised high in the middle of this vast Kingdom. Of course, everyone's thought was to get to the throne. I was so entreated with my surroundings until I found myself not going towards the throne but looking closely at the beautiful crystal-clear golden river lined with trees that people dressed in plain white garments as they cuff the leaves on the trees and smell them. I could hear beautiful music like a surround system, coming up from the ground, so perfect in pitch and all that applies. Interestingly, as I walked on the grass, lovely flowers appeared and as I stepped on them, they would spring back up, as though they were waving at me. I heard Holy, Holy, Holy! Next, I heard, He's Coming, He's Coming! As I continued walking, I came upon a man of the great statue, very distinguish with a beard, and dressed royally! I heard a voice introduce me to Abraham, He said, "This is Annie, she likes to be called Annie Pearl."

Abraham then reached out his hand to welcome me saying, "Hello, Annie, are you thirsty?"

I answered, "Yes!" Then Abraham looked into my eyes and smiled. I felt like the most beautiful woman ever; especially, when I recalled how beautiful Sarah must have been. Abraham offered me a beautiful, jeweled goblet to drink from. I drank from it. He then offered me this round copper-colored fruit, he said, "Eat, so that you may be able to withstand 'The Power Of The Lord'!" I took the largest bite that I could from the fruit, it was so juicy. Abraham gave me the biggest smile for my "out of nowhere humor." It was now time for me to move on with my angel and an unidentified escort(s). We came across a family on a picnic, the mother asked, "Do you want to see our home?"

My escort answered, "She has an appointment with the Lord." My God, as we continued, I was told that the townhouses complex we were coming upon, "This is where the prophets live."

When we got closer, I was asked, "Do you want to see your house?"

I answered, "Yes." However, when we entered, it looked like an old woman lived there. There were flowers everywhere, on the kitchen curtains, table, tablecloth, window sills, sofa, chair, everywhere! I was asked, "What do you think of your house?" All I could think of was, it looks like an old lady lives here, of course, not realizing that I will live to be rightful old age, praise Jehovah. Next, I was asked how I liked a particular table, I realized looking at it that the same designs on Earth are in Heaven. Likewise, because I was sitting in one place not moving around, I was asked, "Do you want to go upstairs?" I looked towards the stairs but remained seated. That's when my escort said, "She wants to be surprised." Perhaps, I will raise the baby I lost, what a surprise that would be. We are now on our way to my divine appointment on the throne. I am now at this vast throne; I see the golden Ark of the Covenant. Hearing Holy, Holy, Holy around the throne and the words He's Coming! I sense there were thousands upon thousands that shared that divine appointment with me; yet I felt it was a one-on-one, as well. Staring upon the throne, the look of a gigantic elevator-like transformer door slides upward, and Jesus appears as if He is coming out of our Heavenly Father, then the grey-colored steel-like door closes. He takes his seat to the right of the Father. Then suddenly, I bowed down at His feet. I see the light of glory shining through the nail holes in His Feet and the light of glory shining through the nail holes in his wrists. Oh, my! The holes were so large. I heard Jesus say to me, "Get up!

Yet, I did not. He said it a second time, Get up! I was thinking to myself, I can't see God and live. Then I heard Jesus say, "That religious spirit!" He said, Get up! I got up.

He said, "I want you to tell your mother, your brothers, and sisters I'm coming back, I'm coming back soon!"

Of course, I agreed to tell them, and I did. I looked around and to my right was a tall candlestick holder with seven candles, I also noticed 24 empty chairs near the throne, as well. I watched as Jesus paced back and forth with great concern for those on earth. Next, I remember Jesus telling my angel to take me back to the mountains, He said, "She loves the mountains," as He smiled so beautifully. Right after hearing those words, my angel and I were boarding the "stagecoach" and leaving via those beautiful mountains. Thinking about my divine encounter, I was all smiles. My angel had the most amazing smile with gorgeous white teeth. All I could do was stare and as I did, he gave me a look of "What is it?" There wasn't anything wrong, I wanted teeth like his, so I gave him a big smile and he smiled back. I felt myself going faster than speed itself, and that is when I awoke in my bed with such awe! I was never the same after that encounter either. I walked around with an awesome glow... I had gone before Almighty God and Jesus.

My Encounter With Hell

I remember talking to God and saying, "Lord, is there a hell? I want to know for sure, so I can tell others." You see, I'd left a denomination that had rewritten the scriptures of the Bible, it was no longer authentic, and its meaning was watered down with no real substance. Therefore, I asked God to show me, if hell exists... but do not leave me there, I just wanted to know. Glory sometime had passed when I made that request of God; however, he honored it when I found myself in this dark, foul-smelling place. There were creatures in cages behind bars reaching for me, as I stood on an island of coal away from the creatures. Some of them still manage to scratch me with their long claws. These creatures showed gnashing of teeth while drooling. The atmosphere was smothering with the smell of thick dense smoke. So dark, at one point, I could not see my hand before me. I started to feel a deep separation from God, this pit was filled with loud screams and noises. I looked up and yelled, "Jesus!" That's when I saw a moving light, like that of a star... I could see what resembled a blue sky from the circular opening at the top of hell. Jesus appeared and (carrying me) took me straight up out of the pit. I was elated, to say the least. Of course, after my encounter with hell, there remain no more doubts... Hell is Real!

A Brief Encounter With Jesus About The Children

I inquired of God about the children in heaven. I wanted to know more about where they lived and more. I saw this large structure, made of light greyish colored bricks with a beautiful, shiny golden dome-shaped top. I saw children of all ages enter and exit the building. I was with Jesus as we looked on from afar. It was obvious that the area was off-limits, and I knew not to inquire about what takes place there. However, I knew these were children who once lived on earth. Interestingly, I noticed there were children of every ethnicity except Asians. I asked the lord why that was. He responded by saying, "They (Asians) did not tell their children about me. I felt a feeling of sadness for Jesus and the children not being taught about God. The encounter ended at that point, I remember waking up saying, "Wow!"

Understanding I Have A God-Ordained Purpose

Interestingly, it was not long after this encounter I stopped dating and decided I wanted Jehovah to do work in me. I wanted my life to be pleasing to him in every area. I wanted to be a virtuous woman in every way. I remember reading my bible more, watching more Christian Networks and spiritual broadcasts, and being intentional about my walk with God. That is, I got more involved in service work at my church, attended conferences, served and ministered the prophetic, attended dreams and visions classes, served as an intercessor, and became a member of Women in Ministry Int'L (WIMI). I now had clarity, direction, and a purpose for living. I could feel the warm blood circulating in my body again, there was nothing cold about my existence. I learned how to love myself more, enjoy my company more than others, and treat myself as royalty because I am. My self-esteem went through the roof as my confidence soared, demonstrating a healthy new mindset. My new outlook on life encouraged me to look at others with compassion, love, and trust, and as a positive friendship. Total freedom to be me around everyone without the shame or guilt of my past. I became a whole healed individual by being honest with myself without blame.

I understand that my Push was getting passed those

negative words, suggestions, behaviors, and forces that were directed toward me by others to discourage me and prevent me from going forward in life. There were times when I experienced sadness, isolation, and great confusion, as to why I would get a negative conversation thrown at me by someone who basks in my encouragement. Really, how could that be? I realized, that not everyone is happy with my progress, my next level, or my shift.

Today, I recall my mom and grandmom being my greatest cheerleaders, although, I encouraged myself a great deal in those days. Likewise, when my greatest supporters passed away, it became more difficult to push myself. You see, my mom and grandmom were always so impressed with my desire to be the best me possible, and I was, during that time in my life. It is important to note, that during the start of my recovery from drugs and alcohol, there were quite a few people who were very unhappy. That is, I wasn't the butt of jokes anymore. My physical appearance improved, as well. Now, I was the focus of a positive lifestyle, with well wishes and congratulations. Therefore, the change in my life forced others to look at themselves. Meaning, that they could no longer hide their dysfunctions, by using and targeting my life as an example.

Clearly, I found "my push" through their pretending, their embarrassment, and their dishonesty toward others. In other words, their disgust to see me win fueled my desire to be motivated and encouraged from within the core of my being. Further, making me realize that I am an overcomer and a dynamic force to be reckoned with in this life. Of course, making it known, I am determined to move forward in every area of my life by being intentional, purposeful, and driven.

Wow, 24 years of freedom from drugs and alcohol feels so incredible, because those substances were in every area of life for over 20+ years. Today, I implement wisdom and biblical principles in my life as a guide for daily living. Spirituality keeps me grounded, that is, knowing that an Almighty God loves me, regardless of me. This is the promise that will carry me through life's challenges for the rest of my blessed life. I have been given another opportunity to appreciate, live, and enjoy life to the fullest. My main focus, as it relates to being a beacon of light to the discouraged and hopeless is mastering my love walk. I sincerely believe that is every person's assignment while living on earth. We must learn to love each other well before we can claim to love the Lover, called Love. My life changed drastically when decided to live as my Heavenly Father requested, that is, to love others as I love myself… including my enemies.

So, you may be asking yourself, "What is the moral of Annie's story?

The moral of my story is, that it doesn't matter if you were born into poverty; were pushed back at every opportunity to keep you from rising above your circumstances; made mistakes in life and were told God doesn't love you anymore; faced disappointments, shame, and guilt; lived a life of alcohol and drugs addiction; experienced the death, separation, and abandonment of a loved one; your body experienced severe chronic pain; you lost cars, houses, money, and other possessions; you were lied on, betrayed, gossiped about, overlooked, joked on, refused access, mistreated, or left to figure it out... You Are Worth Saving!! God can use you for his Glory... You are Loved!! Remember, with all that I have gone through, God never turned His back on me. Our stories are firsthand experiences of how we can unlock the solution to someone's challenges and lead them to freedom. It is very important for me to note that I have made peace within, therefore, I am free to voice my experiences without the dread of others' opinions of me. I am living at a new level of expectancy and manifestation. I walk in pure faith in God, knowing that I will manifest all the promises of God and become who He has called me to be. Life and death are in my mouth, I shall speak positivity and not negativity.

I made a promise to God while I was in active addiction, I said, "Jehovah, if you free me from drugs and alcohol, I promise to write a book and tell everyone about the lies Jehovah's Witnesses (JWs) are proclaiming and why I wanted to kill myself because of their religion." That is, JWs believe they are the one and only true religion; if you make a mistake… you should be disfellowshipped and ostracized from your family and friends; and you are told God doesn't love you, thus, leaving you with no one to turn to spiritually." This is a whole LIE!! Do Not Fall For This Lie!! Grateful my family did not turn their backs on me.

First of all, there is nothing a person can do to separate themselves from the love of God. God is Love. God promised to never leave us nor forsake us. God is not mad at us. God is not looking to harm us in any way… The Devil wants to steal, kill, and destroy us Not God! Our God is loving, caring, compassionate, and understanding, and sees the beauty in and around us.

Likewise, I have kept my promise to God (Jehovah) to tell the world, God loves us, and no one can stop it… we cannot stop God from loving and protecting us from the enemy. Rise up from every low place of hopelessness, loneliness, depression, oppression, stagnation, defeat, and doubt. Come up and receive your joy, happiness, abundance, victory, blessings, breakthroughs, healings, and opportunities. I am grateful that everything the enemy sends our way is being turned around by God and used for our good and not evil. I am excited about my future because I did not let the enemy stop me from obeying God. I am excited about your future too because God is exalted. The devil is a liar. And because God is The Greatest power, we shall never be defeated. May the Love of God keep you grateful, thankful, humble, and blessed. Much love, my friend. More, Abundant, Grace!

ABOUT THE AUTHOR

Annie P. Rivers' goal is to encourage and to build hope, confidence, and self-esteem in the lives of those hurting, and for whatever reason, feel God does not love them. She is a recovering person with 25 years of freedom from drugs and alcohol. An extended amount of Annie's career has been served in the field of Substance Abuse and Prevention in the following capacities: Behavioral Health Prevention Specialist (COSA-NCADD); Certified Recovery Trainer and Coach; Certified Peer Support Specialist (CPSS); and Associate Prevention Specialist (APS). Annie is excited about reaching more individuals in need of assistance as more future opportunities become available.